*No Texting at the Dinner Table*

*Also by Christopher Goodrich*

*Nevertheless, Hello* (2009, Steel Toe Books)
*By Reaching* (2007, Finishingline Press)

# No Texting at the Dinner Table

## Christopher Goodrich

The New York Quarterly Foundation, Inc.
New York, New York

NYQ Books™ is an imprint of The New York Quarterly Foundation, Inc.

The New York Quarterly Foundation, Inc.
P. O. Box 2015
Old Chelsea Station
New York, NY 10113

www.nyq.org

Copyright © 2014 by Christopher Goodrich

All rights reserved. No part of this book may be used or reproduced in any manner whatsoever without written permission of the author except in the case of brief quotations embodied in critical articles and reviews.

First Edition

Set in New Baskerville

Layout by Joseph Hamersly

Cover Illustration: ©istockphoto.com/robeo

Author Photo by Cliff Lynn

Library of Congress Control Number: 2014945816

ISBN: 978-1-935520-77-1

*No Texting at the Dinner Table*

# *Acknowledgements*

*Cider Press Review:* "Pickers"
*Diner:* "On Being Rejected from Diner Magazine for the Fourth Time"
*Entelechy International:* "Before the Wedding"
*Fledgling Rag:* "The Miscarriage," "After Emily Bronte's Spellbound," "Simile"
*Main Street Rag:* "Witnessing the Success of Others"
*Margie:* "The Blame Game (for ages 3 and up)"
*Natural Bridge:* "Confronting Plagiarism"
*The New York Quarterly:* "Charles Shultz, 1922-2000"
*Ocho:* "To My Cheating Ex-Girlfriend, On Her Wedding Day"
*PFS Post:* "In the Event of an Emergency," "The State of Our Art"
*Rattle:* "Telling the Truth to Daughters," "Peeing After the Movie"
*The Binnacle:* "For My Daughter, When She is Born"

# Contents

*In a Dress, In a Dream*

The Miscarriage  /15
We Do Not Yet Have a Child  /16
The Blame Game (for ages 3 and up)  /17
What's Missing  /18
After Emily Bronte's Spellbound  /19
For My Daughter, When She is Born  /20

*A Kind of Living*

Courage  /23
Cheating the Dentist  /24
About Feet  /25
Laughing at Cancer  /26
The New Amazon  /27
Mother  /28
Watching Sex Scenes with Your Parents When You're Quite Young  /29

*Truth and Daughters*

I Wake Up to the Sound of My Wife, 4 Months Pregnant, Crying  /33
Tracking the Progress of My Wife's Dilating Cervix  /34
The Possibility of Poop  /36
Misnomer  /37
H  /38
Telling the Truth to Daughters  /39
Should Juliet Awaken in Time  /40
Advice on Advice  /42

### 7th Period Legs

How to Convince Her You're the One   /*45*
The First I Love You   /*46*
Problem Solving   /*48*
Before the Wedding   /*49*
One Spoon   /*50*
The Marriage of Q and U   /*51*

### Pull Up a Chair

To My Cheating Ex-Girlfriend, On Her Wedding Day   /*55*
Blindness, and the Theory that it's Linked to Masturbation   /*56*
Divorce Club   /*57*
In the Event of an Emergency   /*58*
Charles Shultz, 1922-2000   /*59*
Paul McCartney Turns 64   /*60*
It's a Wonderful Life II; Clarence Gets His Wings   /*62*

### One Stoic Heron

F.D. Reeve Invites Us to Lunch   /*65*
On Being Rejected From Diner Magazine For the Fourth Time   /*67*
Witnessing the Success of Others   /*68*
The State of Our Art, 2007   /*69*

*Coco-Cola and Brotherhood*

Pickers  /*73*
Confronting Plagiarism  /*74*
Inner City English  /*75*
Simile  /*76*
Renaldo  /*77*
To the Jules E. Mastbaum High School Student Who Positioned Me
       8th on His Hit List.  /*78*
When You're Late  /*79*
After Reading Grace Paley, I'm Inspired to Write a Short Poem  /*80*
Walking In  /*81*
Peeing After the Movie  /*82*

*for Mayzie and Leilah and Penelope*
*a truth.*

*In a Dress, In a Dream*

# The Miscarriage

*Thanksgiving 2007*

The card we composed looked like your handwriting—
that was the point—two smiling stick figures
holding blue balloons announcing your arrival—
we drove two and a half hours south
to tell your grandmother, who, when we arrived,
sliced apples, splashed cinnamon.
Your grandfather carved the bird, jumped up and up,
cried *this is the world, this is the only world,*
though soon after the football game we knew the bleeding
and emergency room, the RN who couldn't find the vein in your mother's arm
and the no no nono and me reading Entertainment Weekly
in between trips to the bathroom to see if her spotting disappeared
and a second nurse, Joanna I think, holding my hand,
directing me to the cafeteria to remember the smell
of something simmering, telling me to bring back bottled water
for both of us.

But forget all that. For the moment, let's go back
to the allspice and honeyed ham, the pyramid
of twice baked potatoes, the onioned gravy
and unexpected hugging, even the cranberry sauce
still in the shape of the can which I usually can't stomach,
the bread buttered and buttered, the family asking the personal questions,
telling the private stories—all of us learning one another,
removed from our shared divisiveness and disappointment
and later, gathered around the television with our chamomile
and pumpkin pie and our fists in the air and our tongues
shouting homemade hallelujahs, betting on the game,
howling for the Redskins, who we knew didn't stand a chance.
We rooted for them. We rooted for them anyway.

## We Do Not Yet Have a Child

hammering the porcelain night—1:36am,
2:13am, 3:49am, 5:15am, forcing us
to secure the kitchen cabinets, reminding us
of us—we do not yet know who we are.

No gum giddy grin, no drooling gremlin
to push in a door frame swing. We do not
yet lie under the storm of such joy—
the projectile poop, the footsy pajamas.

We haven't learned what it is
to be that kind of human,
to love that wide and often.

# The Blame Game (for ages 3 and up)

*Contents:* 1 Dysfunctional Family, 1 Score Card, 1 Blame Game Ball with 6 inch Detachable Spikes, Inestimable Rage.

*Game Play:* 5 Players form a circle. Mother, Father, Sister, Brother and You. Player 1 throws ball to any other Player within the circle while yelling a past regret for which he/she refuses to take responsibility. If unsure of what to yell, you may try: "Who are you to blame me for Grandma's death? I only stepped out of the house for a minute." Or "Maybe if you stop drinking, Dad will come home." Should Player 2 catch the ball, once thrown, it is safe to assume he/she has internalized your guided/misguided hatred and must quickly, because no one can hold such a thing for very long, throw to another Player within the circle while yelling louder than the previous Player. If, upon consensus, any Player's blame is not equal to or greater than the blame of a previous Player, he/she is out. Should anyone within the circle drop the ball, or catch the ball but refuse to accept the blame, becoming then, argumentative and unseemly, he/she must leave the circle, in fact the house, in fact the family, thinking of what he/she has done. If, once packed and gone, this player dies by thunder, thirst, hail, snow, flood, hurricane, tornado, or a UV index above 7, and the remaining players are riddled with enough guilt, the deceased player wins the entire game. Continue until 1 is left standing. Obscenities are welcome and encouraged. (Note: You may insert optional 12 inch spikes.)

## What's Missing

The poem I'm not writing is sensational.
You would fall in love with me, I'm sure,
should you read it. A thing I can't chance.
Not at this juncture. Not with my heart
promised to a Canadian with dibs on my babies.

I can tell you my mother is involved,
certain non-negotiable complications,
a refrain that would slow your heart
to reveal what's missing,
an ending so sweet, you would swear
every moment before it was lonelier than the last.

You would question your values,
as I question my own.
Those I have been handed, that is,
by people I'm no longer talking to;
this fact startles me above all others.
I say it better in the poem I'm not writing.

There is a cleverness to the poem
you'd begin to despise. It's a good thing,
after all, that it doesn't exist. I should know.
I've been trying to write it for years.
I believe I am lost without it. I believe,
should I ever find it, I will lose you too.

## After Emily Bronte's Spellbound

The night consumes our daylight,
the city breaks in two,
one of us will leave tonight
but it will not be you.

Hold fast, my love, your woolen cape,
devastation's crawling through,
one of us will find escape
but it cannot be you.

Heaven bids you see this—
that desperate thing you knew,
only one of us can flee this
and it will not be you.

# For My Daughter, When She is Born

You came to me in a dress, in a dream
with cloud bitten ankles, and though
I don't remember the color (white I think,
something yellowy and floral about the edges),
it was clear you were standing, as was I,
your hand touching my face, telling me
to calm, to breathe, you'd wait indefinitely
until it was time. And when I hold your
bloody body for the first time, your startled pinkness
protruding from the hospital blanket, the both of us
listening to the light from whence you came,
I'll ask because I need to know
what it's like in that place, up there,
in that other waiting room, what you remember,
before you grow too accustomed to this light
and, like everyone else, forget, little heart.

*A Kind of Living*
───────────────────────

# Courage

See that little girl sitting,
bologna sandwich, freckles,
feet swinging above the ground?

See, a few benches away,
that little boy, waiting, watching,
his hands wringing,

standing up, sitting down
standing up, sitting down?

## Cheating the Dentist

I am not the type to lie. Which is a lie.
I am not the kind to begin flossing
3 nights before the appointment
so he'll think I've been flossing
since he and I last shook hands. Lie.
Anyone can see that my gums
are chewed and bleeding. Oh yes, Dr. Dentist
I brush 3 times a day, pop sugarless gum,
rinse with Listerine every
morning so my co-workers think
my mouth naturally smells like this.
Sure, I chew food 36 times before swallowing—
I really did try this once—Brush
too hard? Love too little? Positively.
Embarrassed by government,
the string of saliva hanging
post-kiss? Who I am after the job
has lowered my standards? You
want to know why I keep my tonsils?
I'm terrified, that's why. I don't want to die.

## About Feet

I married a woman who has them.
And though I mostly love this woman—
she imbibes a kind of wonder
that crawls constantly under my skin—
god help me when, beneath
our working class covers
she rubs those icy pillars of certain death
across my warming calves.
It too is a kind of living I know—
a kind with which I want nothing to do—
for I can't help but leap under the red duvet
to the outer edge of our full bed,
crying and cursing—
a kind of singing of the happily married—
and because I also have these feet
on wintry occasions, these polar piggies
no one wants, she reminds me,
sometimes several times in one day,
that I, too, am someone
to love.

## Laughing at Cancer

I know cancer as well as anyone
who's read Donald Hall.
That is to say not really. Nor do I know
why Tony chose to call and tell me first—
he has closer friends. But he did so
after I left, once the dinner was over,
spoke of his shot libido,
how he has no dick left. The cancer,
he says, broke open like clapping. Even as I write
is swallowing his 3rd and 4th vertebrae.
Soon his brain. Next his family. Then everything he owns.
Earlier, we ate crab cakes, chowder. We reminisced.
I hugged his wife and daughter.
And this wasn't helpless hugging,
this was happy hugging, twice.
I hadn't seen him in ten years.
Though once driving away, south on 270,
the phone rings and I'm listening
when I can and when he is done talking, he is done
except for a kind of laughter I'd never heard before,
a kind of laughter you could build a house with,
if you like curtained windows,
a garbage disposal and new cellar door.
If you like a TV in every room
to keep your loved ones occupied.

# The New Amazon

Customers who bought Stephen King
may also enjoy Mary Higgins Clark,
James Patterson, and Stephen King
just as customers who purchased summer
squash might also like snow peas, broccoli,
swinging as an adult. Those who prefer childhood,
may also enjoy cherry bank lollipops,
and never looking back.  And those who bought
never looking back will certainly, one day, die,
and wish they had remembered an old house,
a letter written in cursive.  Those who bought one love
may buy another. Just as popular are short yellow skirts,
the memory of an ex, a woman you owe
with a ticking uterus. Those who bought one home:
debt, security, a fence needing repair, and those
who bought housework: a family, then, a family running away.
Customers who bought the war on terror may also enjoy
the war on melancholy, the war on itchiness and the war
on hotdogs. This is how easy it is to buy something,
with an eye on something else.
Another chardonnay, tighter jeans, this perfume,
that convertible. Doesn't that belong on our mantle,
and won't this look nice when we awake
to sunlight? Though if you like sun, you may also enjoy
an afternoon memorizing Shakespeare, no wallet,
no new toaster, instead: a hike with your daughter,
a conversation with thunder.

# Mother

How odd to discover
that I am my mother
in the kitchen—a fact pointed out
by my now wife, who,
if I am to judge, cannot
do *it* as well as mother or me
—boiling milk, basting the roast—
it doesn't matter what *it* is,
and though I've tried
to teach her, as gently as I can,
how best to stir fry tofu,
she will never, to her own detriment,
listen, in the kitchen. My wife thinks
I'm the controlling one
which is an insult, let's be honest,
to the woman who raised me,
the only one who can make
the tuna noodle casserole
an ambrosia, the first woman
to love me through tacos,
to show me how to win
an argument with quiche,
which is, ironically, what
I must make here, now,
if Rachel will kindly let me
take the reigns, the spatula,
in order to save, once again,
our marriage.

# Watching Sex Scenes with Your Parents When You're Quite Young

I forgive my nervous mother,
my uneasy step-father,
though fast forwarding
was, no doubt, an option
and yet, I trust it was our fortune
to sit in that red rush of a silence,
paralyzed, acknowledging together
what happens in certain locked rooms
of the world—a kind of growing up
no one can escape. And to those
who don't appreciate suffering,
to those who haven't tasted
the dank sick salt of maturation, I say:
try watching Demi Moore go down
on Michael Douglas in the glow
of a moaning summer evening
with your sweatered mother sitting
next to you smelling of dried fruit,
your step-father foaming
at the mouth. There are moments
we cannot help but tremble through.
Do not breathe. Do not make a sound.
Eye contact will kill you. Some sweat
sticks forever to our frail and frightened faces.

*Truth and Daughters*

# I Wake Up to the Sound of My Wife, 4 Months Pregnant, Crying

Before sleep, she turns her body toward mine—
an act more difficult now then it once was—
her belly pulsing with someone whose name I do not know—
and asks, *do you still think I'm sexy?*
And the truth, without permission, without
thinking this one out, put on its tapping shoes
and hit the floor.

Rachel, I am not always the husband
I promised to be. I am working through this.
Remember when I arrived home
Monday night, tired, achy, pissed at parents
for forgetting our fundraising meeting
and didn't I still walk Seamus in the 28 degree chill?
Didn't I shovel the driveway three times
that day when the ice masked our little street
like a metaphor? Didn't I touch you all night after that
and open the window to let the cool air in?

Perhaps none of this matters now. I know I left
for work the next morning without waking you to say goodbye.
I am still in awe that you feel happy and safe
in our bed, under our covers, carrying that child.

Sometimes it is all I can do to close my eyes,
reach my hand to your quiet, sleeping face.
I can't tell you what life is now that this child
is wearing your beautiful body,
feeding on your mind and temperament,
wrapped in your heart and lungs.

# Tracking the Progress of My Wife's Dilating Cervix

5 cm
The nurse on call reads the business end
of my exposed wife—5 centimeters
last she checked—a figure that reminds,
with unwavering certainty,
I am no longer 21, no longer leaving
for New York City in the morning,
never again waking some 2am without wondering
if I locked the door, turned off the oven, secured the baby gate.
The nurse shakes my hand. Her skin is moist.

6 cm
It's difficult to remember
my last sit-down meal
that didn't require shouting
a combo number into a speaker.
I can't remember the color of the tablecloths,
the name of the waitress.
Did she call me sir?
Did I have dessert?
Oh dear Lord, I can't remember,
DID I HAVE DESSERT?

7 cm
A lesson: My wife has never loved anything
more than this yet-to-be someone. Not you.
Not me. The dog and I are becoming inseparable
friends. I buy him treats. He eats them.

8 cm
I have never loved anything more
than this yet-to-be someone. Not you.
Not me. Not even the dog, who knows
some disaster is ahead.

9 cm
Pediatrician? Check. Day care provider? Check.
Car seat inspection? Check. Cord blood donation?
Check. CPR training? Shit.
Uncontrollable whimpering?
More than you're ready for.

10 cm
Little girl, I will learn fire.
I will teach you how.

# The Possibility of Poop

During delivery, I mean.
There was a chance
I would see my wife poop.
We had even discussed it
beforehand, how scared
she was that with the head
of the child would come
the head of something else—
as if the world could not
bestow beauty alone.
Some balance underscored
every glory.  But the baby
was, how to say this, not
beautiful either, she hadn't
yet earned it. Far too gray
and red in funny places,
more orifices than is
possible spitting pus
and a cone head. I mean
this girl had a real cone
head. And we loved that
ugly thing, we knew
it would become human
in minutes before our eyes.
Soon as she looked at us,
we knew her. And, Darling,
not an inch of poop.
Though even if there was
I wouldn't say because
I love you and I'd like you
to continue to love me
and poop sometimes
gets in the way of love
if you let it, if you admit to it,
if you admit to it every time.

# Misnomer

Whoever coined the phrase
*sleep like a baby* has never, guaranteed,
spent significant time with a baby,
much less slept with one nearby.
If he had, he would know this story:
the relief of watching baby fall asleep
at mama's breast, the superhuman feat
of putting one hand below baby's head,
one hand below the trunk, carrying baby to her crib
without waking her. He would know the unparalleled terror
of slowly, gingerly lowering baby to her own mattress,
begging God for another favor. He would taste the fear
of tiptoeing back to his own bed, hardly breathing,
unable to risk a blink. He would suffer
the uncertainty of climbing underneath his own covers,
raising them noiselessly, wrapping
his strained and beaten body. And once he has
given himself fully to the mattress, the second he relaxes,
the very moment he releases the day's tension,
he would know the familiar full throttle cry
beckoning him back to replace the pacifier.
There is nothing resembling sleep here.
This baby, for one reason or another,
wants you dead, is in cahoots with the witch doctor next door,
whose fender you dented four years ago. She is 16 pounds.
26 inches long with approximately 1.5 teeth.
And she will not stop until you've paid for every last infraction.
She knows where you live, who you love.
She is the most terrifying thing you've ever adored.

# H

Suppose, one evening, you find yourself
hovering above our bed, the master bedroom
ensconced by a ghostly summer dusk,
and you have the presence of mind
to peer down at my sleeping family.
You might think we were sponsored
by the letter H—two strong parental posts
bisected by my daughter's beating body,
her sweaty head molded firmly to my wife's torso,
her feet attached to my lower spine.
You might assume we were the beginning
of some *Happiness*, or, if you too have lived
this literature, *Help*, but in truth, we stand
for nothing, though *Hell* comes to mind,
and *Heaven* is not out of the question. Tonight,
we are simply three people sleeping away
what remains of the day, one of us transitioning seamlessly
into morning, the other two, in our half sleep,
in our quarter sleep, no doubt, thanking good glory
for caffeine and Tylenol and that big beautiful yellow bus,
which will take her away, bring her back.

## Telling the Truth to Daughters

There comes a time when even daughters
must give themselves, open mouthed,
open bodied to the tongue of a boy, knowing
he will lick what he likes,
and I (dear god) must approve. How
can I not and continue to respect myself?
Hasn't sex with other men's daughters
gotten me this far? Doesn't the world
owe some pleasure to my own?
Doesn't everyone deserve even this?

I will tell her the truth (oh god), that…that…
this too is right—wild sex when you're young and firm
with a boy you know and love. Even (oh my god)
with a boy you will never know, never love—
it can be mind-numbing, brilliant—usually (dear lord, dear god in heaven)
even more so.

## Should Juliet Awaken in Time

Dazed, but breathing, the only
sound in the tomb the quiet beast
of a shell-shocked Romeo, they
return to Verona, living
one week with her parents
one week with his, hers, his, hers
and Romeo, who has waved goodbye
to the ninth grade forever,
makes himself useful
in some technical vocation—
an auto mechanic's assistant,
or no, yes, a cabinet maker,
apprentice to the cabinet mak—no,
a part time temp in a textile mill,
pouring coffee, making copies—
and at 15, Juliet's body still reels
from giving birth—the autistic child
gets little benefit as such—
and both sit feverishly home
on evenings past 9 without
speaking, two who knew perfectly
how to die not knowing how
to live, support themselves, each other,
an open window delivering
the sounds of more and less
fortunate Veronians and the bawling baby
in daddy's arms does not want the breast,
the bassinet, refuses coddling
and Romeo's sleep-deprived eyes,
wondering how best to stop the screaming,
dart from baby to open window,
baby to window, baby
to window and Juliet's from Romeo to baby,
Romeo to baby, Romeo to window
which is now closed, latched—

Juliet exiting with the child
and Romeo, who is not used
to answering phones, taking
messages, massages aching
hands with aching hands.

## Advice on Advice

The best you can give, at 2:27am,
to your in-sickness-or-in-health wife
whose nipples are chapped, who's rocked
for an hour, your whimpering, deflated
second child, who leaks from one eye, whose
indiscernible blaspheming carries with it
the clear repetition of your Christian name,
who sharpens into a stake a sippy-cup on the bottom post
of your marriage bed, who, when you awake,
is chanting over fire, sacrificing a mountain goat,
the best advice you can give at a time like this,
is no advice at all. I found this out on Tuesday evening,
last week. Best not to begin with:
*What I would do is, and you need to calm*
*down because.* And speaking from experience,
death will certainly do you part sooner
if you do what appears the sensible, rational,
understated, respectful bowing out, and return to sleep.
This, perhaps, is worse than any advice you
could have given in the first place. I found this out
on Wednesday evening, last week. Shut up and stay awake.
Sit with your back to the headboard,
starring, focused, ahead. Study the lesson with the intensity
of a college freshman. There is paper and pencil
on the bedside table. Take Cornell notes.
Stay afterwards to ask questions. Be the first to arrive
next time. Raise your hand before speaking.
Never, not ever again, not ever ever again
ask to use the bathroom during class.
Tell her, when everyone else departs,
it was your lack of medication that caused the disruption,
and tomorrow you will bring a doctor's note,
the prescription itself, and the introduction
to your work-in-progress dissertation, the thesis of which
has something to do with the sexual cannibalism
of certain insects: A male's survival rate post copulation.

# *7th Period Legs*

# How to Convince Her You're the One

If you spend hours plotting
the perfect mix of charm, strength
and sexy, if you must avoid her
to get her to say in passing
to a friend, *Who's that, I want him,*
if you must pretend at the end
of the phone call that *No, it's ok,
I have to go too,* if you are, at this instant,
combing Sinatra with Tori Amos lyrics, reading
Weiner novels, spending more than 40 minutes
searching for the purple Care Bear
her 2 year old daughter longs for,
in short, if you must convince her
you're the one, you're not the one.
Get over it. Your friends are waiting.

## The First I Love You

It was more question than conviction,
my voice rose on the final syllable,
and when it's out there, look the hell out.
I remember we touched, Allison and I,
but only our foreheads. Hands in our pockets,
we stared at cold tile below, the foyer of her house
chilled and stone, the faint smell of left over Chow Mein,
the front door cracked open behind us, my body
an erection, my erection an erection,
my engine an engine revving. It was what happened next
that replaced my heart with tin foil, the silence afterwards
I mean. The gaping, suffocating, wound in the air
a one two three punch life-threatening and fierce,
a sudden wind in the foyer, a tornado of dry wall and staircase.
Wondering, *Did she hear me? Should I say it again?*
*Perhaps, once more before leaving?* The path between
house door and car door a fire walk,
driving the longest road home, if I could remember
home, what it looked like, if it existed,
if I could remember how to drive, what were keys,
did I own a car and so forth.

This may happen to you, Mayzie. The boy
hopefully, an exact replica of me, because I'm
amazing (you deserve amazing),
and it might be in this very house when the two of you
are alone after Chow Mein and then the conclusive
and hammering nothing after an ill-timed *I Love You*.
And he might go home, if he can find his home, his car, the road
and so forth, threaten his parents, never speak to you again
or text you again or whatever it is you do to communicate
with potential lovers in 15 years, or worse, call everyday, every hour.
I am here to tell you this:
There will be no texting at the dinner table. You know how
I hate it. That is our time. Your mother gets home late enough as it is.
He will grow up, trust me, to find a girl to marry, 10 years later.

They will make a baby who will or will not
love a boy. That is what love is: the sickening scent
of left over Chow Mein and never calling again.
Love is finding language and using language
and love is silence like a fist and love is shaping
that silence into a knife and threatening
those you love most. Does any of this make sense?
If you need to speak to someone about how and what
you're felling, and I'm not around, and mommy is working,
call Allison, she knows: 301-665-3283.
Tell her how you feel. I did. Look where it's gotten me.
It's gotten me to you.

## Problem Solving

Through Mr. Mordenski's windowless hole
of a math class, his backwater stare, hair wrapping
from god knows where, one after another
I solve them—a painful procedure
when dealing with numbers, those elliptic
harmonic dysfunctions, and why I despise 7th period.
Why I cheat every chance I get.

If closer attention is paid, if I respect
$\Pi$ and its connection to my disappointment,
appreciate the geometric topology
of a perfect circle, memorize
each complex differential operator,
would I be so paralyzed
by Allison Warshof's 7th period legs,
a pair of legs toned from 6th period gym,
wondering why she doesn't call,
gritting my teeth to nubbins, causing more problems
than I, with my 7th period mind, can solve?

And after digesting my fill of linear algebra—
two matrices intersecting a bi-vector space,
the quadratic agreement between Allison and myself,
4 legs, if I count properly, could I cancel,
as we are taught, one variable from our too complicated equation?
Can I walk out on those legs forever?
It's difficult to say. I am an English major.
Right and wrong are not welcome
in our nebulous vocabulary. We don't
solve problems. We write essays on Man vs Nature,
and, when we are ready, Man vs Man.

## Before the Wedding

Before the wedding,
the wedding rehearsal
and before rehearsing,
months of coming
and going, missing each other
less and less. Who's
to say who loves whom,
or if we dare at all?
Today, I haven't loved
anybody, haven't missed
a soul and I regret
telling you so. Please
don't take this the wrong way,
my love, my future,
it is only the truth.
Besides, now you
know me, truly, and isn't that
(forgive me)
what you wanted.

# One Spoon

When one marries, finally,
after a year and a half
of asking what napkin
matches what bouquet,
does one begin dreaming
of Elizabeth Fisher, the girl,
age 16, who offered to share,
can you imagine, her brownie sundae,
one spoon?

I collect Elizabeth Fishers
the way the world collects
missing children—one
faded photograph at a time,
on a discarded milk carton,
the caption Have You Seen Me?
hovering somewhere above.
It's too late for fudge
Elizabeth, but I still wonder
in dreams, where you are.
It's late. You're beginning to worry me.

# The Marriage of Q and U

You'd never guess, seeing them now,
how miserable they once were—
Q with his quick temper,
U with her love for the useless—

how handsome he was as a lower
case—the round head of someone
important, the skinny, sturdy body.
And u like a cup of kindness,

those curves, that little tail.
Now grown, she hasn't changed a bit.
Just taller, wider in the waist.
But Q is something else altogether—

plump with a tiny prick.
There were those who said
it wouldn't work. Rumors
abounded of Q and A

running here together, running there.
But the wedding was just
as they pictured:
P and R presiding over Q,

U given away by T and V.
And afterwards, they were
never apart, nestled quiet
in the quilt of their union,

the unquestioned quality of it.

*Pull Up a Chair*
_____

# To My Cheating Ex-Girlfriend, On Her Wedding Day

In my dreams I play flower girl
at your wedding. A meticulous
and rehearsed walk down
the lantern-lit aisle, a white wicker
basket anchoring my enthusiasm,
releasing the pink petals carelessly
into the wind. Pink being, in my mind,
the color of grace, the basket a symbol of sanity,
my dress, black as a bitch slap, the only sign
that something is terribly wrong.

That and the fact that I kidnapped,
in the name of forgiveness, the real flower girl,
tied her to the back seat of my car
(Don't worry, I've cracked the windows). She'll return
home after the reception, unharmed,
I promise, after we have danced and danced,
and after, god willing, I lift a glass to you Jennifer,
to you Chris, that you both may see how much I have grown.

## Blindness, and the Theory that it's Linked to Masturbation

Because I'm not seeing as well as I've seen,
it's easy to wonder,
has it something to do with my morning routine?

In the wee hours waking out of a dream,
my body a siphon of spittle and thunder,
I'm no longer seeing as well as I've seen.

Contours and colors have lost their pristine,
the faces of friends are falling asunder,
I fear it's because of my morning routine.

What can be done to retain the world's sheen?
Abstain from this habit? Watch pleasure plunder!
I'm simply not seeing as well as I've seen.

True, I'm no longer that strapping machine
who would burst at the sight of a moist tangerine.
Perhaps I should change my morning routine,

though, loving myself is more than it seems,
I'm certain it's all of this pressure I'm under.
I long for the days when I was sixteen.
I'm no longer seeing as well as I've seen.

# Divorce Club

Welcome. Thank you for coming.
Pull up a chair. No, not that one,
the other one. Yes. Good. Comfortable?
Don't put your feet on the table. Ever.
Something to drink? Lemonade, you say?
I'll get you a glass of water. Very good tap here.
Okay! A book? I love that one too.
We don't have it. Self Help mostly. You'd like one
of those? I have none to recommend.
I see you've brought a journal. Sharing
is for another time. Well, mostly we sit and try
to accommodate. Sometimes discussion groups.
Today's topic: Getting What You Want Every Time.
What's that? No, no, go ahead, ask for anything,
anything. Yes, I wish that were possible too.

## In the Event of an Emergency

When the oxygen masks drop,
I will apply one first to my own mouth,
as we were instructed, make sure
I am still alive, before helping you
with yours. In this moment,
according to the government,
I am most important.
This admission is the only way
to ensure your survival. If you need
assistance, you must acknowledge
that I will always come first.
Your life may depend upon it.

# Charles Shultz, 1922-2000

How often have I imagined
Charlie Brown kicking that fucking football,
caressing Lucy's cherubic face,
the two of them making out there in the dirt,
the two of them getting it right?
It never happened that way
and now it never will. We must
live with this everyday
for the rest of our lives. Waking up
isn't difficult, it's facing another,
the suspicion of those who say
*let me hold this for you.*
Running as we must, kicking the air,
free-falling, then the fist of dry dust clogging
our weakened sinuses.
It is, by now, trite to sing
God bless you Charlie Brown
for knowing it was possible,
for believing in something bigger
than Lucy, for wanting to kick
the hell out of something, just once.
And, Lucy, I'm reevaluating your pathetic role
in all of this. Every year I watch you on television,
that truth in your eyes, that wink in your voice,
and you convince me too
that "maybe this time, maybe this time…"
I say it every morning now.

# Paul McCartney Turns 64

Though it's a different 64
than he'd have us believe.
No hair loss. No needing
feeding. His aging is a luxury,

a rarity among rock royalty,
meaning, if necessary,
someone will feed him,
he can afford it, but not

the shepard's pie or chili dog
that you and I are used to.
His is the New York Strip
marinated in lemon peel

and sapphire. The Lobster
Bisque which says genius,
which says 64 is a year
to sing about. Tomorrow

is my birthday too Paul, an event
that may be insignificant
in the eyes of rock audiences
but a miracle, no less.

The thrumming of the afterlife
calling us both home.
With any luck, with any justice,
you will die first, you've earned it.

But not before I settle down
with a band of my own—wife, child
and not before I have enough
in my pocket to, one of these days

I swear, send you a valentine,
a mature merlot. I will do
all these things and more:
drive your car, carry that weight

because I still need you, Paul.
But I will not feed you.
Not even if you asked.
Well maybe, maybe if you asked.

# It's a Wonderful Life II; Clarence Gets His Wings

Now the party's over, dancing's done.
The Baileys lie fast asleep
in their new thousands, and way up north,
way up, the official ceremony—

crab dip, angel food cake.
And because it's Hollywood,
bouncing bare-breasted angels
giggle and dote. We feel the glitter,

the glam. We hear the wings
thwack tight to the shoulders—heavier
than he imagined and rough for feathers.
The infinite weight forever fixed—

the burden of love, the boredom
of success. And given all the bright light
the squinting alone may kill him.
His acceptance speech mentions none of this.

He is blushing, kind. Thanks all
who made it possible, says he can't wait
to fly, when someone interrupts,
one of the big wigs, laughing from the back,

*They're only decorative, you ol' card,*
and Clarence, laughing too,
pauses, nervous, says *Thank you*
again and retreats to his room.

It's difficult, as you can imagine,
to undress. And what with bell after bell
echoing from Earth, nearly impossible
to sleep. In the morning,

he will rise, but stiffly this time, stiffly,
the angel in him screaming with pain.

*One Stoic Heron*

## F.D. Reeve Invites Us to Lunch


We talked turkey,
of all things, wet with gravy

someone said: how the mouth waters
before the bite, when, from the shoulder,

the grouse, I can't tell you how confident,
broke into terrible flight, shattering

the windshield of the SUV in front of ours,
exploding then into the thick unforgiving

Maryland humidity. I did not,
as might become another driver—

there were others, after all, with me—
stop the car at once, at all.

I did not get out to remove what was left
from the road, I jerked the wheel right, slamming

simultaneously the brake, avoiding
by inches, the bloodied body,

the dangling heart. One of us
hit her head hard against the glass.

When, years later, we arrived,
I ate the meat as those around me did,

participated, when I could, in conversation,
dipped the cherry tomatoes in chilled ranch,

ate the tender chicken skin first,
my mouth moist as suicide. Over and again

I dipped those ripe tomatoes,
biting clean through, their tiny explosions

a matter I couldn't consider. I had, god protect me,
my own dreams to lose. I didn't know which ones would go first.

# On Being Rejected From Diner Magazine For the Fourth Time

It is, by now, painfully obvious
the beef is overdone. A shame,
the lettuce seems to have wilted

months ago, the ketchup squeezed
from diseased maggot-rich tomatoes.
But think of this:

You have been traveling. The turkey club
has escaped you all year.
Maybe you haven't touched Worcester

since your mother died.
Maybe the Kamikaze Burger
pictured charmingly on the menu

has called from the pit of your soul:
vidalia onions, twice aged cheddar, bacon
like a wet dream, garlic-glazed sauerkraut,

two dollops of wasabi paste
and a hickory-smoked finish.
The pickle, kosher-crisp.

Only a beautiful waitress,
smiling in all the right places,
announces they have none today,

brings you yesterday's blue plate.
Perhaps she's sick of your mother,
her skin fragile as distant music,

her aching feet refusing to refill your coke.

# Witnessing the Success of Others

I wish it were different, this overwhelming
momentary impulse to pour acid into the eyes
of my dearest friends, people I've shared meals with
over candlelight, whose husbands I've hugged,
my friends, who have book deals before I do.
Recently, a colleague appeared in *The American Poetry Review*,
his name statuesque and limitless on the cover,
and sure I emailed him admitting his deserved celebration,
champagne, a DJed house party, he's one of the nicest
men I know, but not before, I'm afraid, I secretly
wished all those he loved buried alive, his house
ransacked by angry neutered bulls. I'm not usually
like this. My heart sings Gershwin, my soul
organizes soup kitchens. I hate myself for it—
the flippant prayer for these loved ones, loved ones
whose children I've baptized, to inherit a gout-ridden
grandmother, a venereal disease. Alice James
just announced publication of a dear poet, someone
whose work I admire, someone I came to know
over summer and scrabble, someone I regret,
I've already taken to a forest in my mind
and covered with poisoned honey. I would never kill her.
But I might leave her, disoriented with alcohol,
to find her own way home some 20 degree evening
through a path populated by starving Grizzlies.
Sure I settle down, even grow happy, even joyous,
even brilliant with satisfaction at the way my own life
has turned out, my wife and I trying for children,
our new condo opening like a prayer onto a magnificent lake.
The ducks, the geese, the one stoic heron who has seen this man
inside of me, who flies away every time he approaches.

# The State of Our Art, 2007

Upon the anticipated arrival
of the new journal
in which I appear, I slowly savor
my own poem, maybe two,
three times (I even read
my biography) before shelving it,
satisfied that my existence
exists. Like the author
who enters the bookstore
to find himself on the shelf
without noticing his neighbors;
I often look into the eyes of strangers
I pass on the highway
not to see who shares the road,
but more and more,
to see if I am seen.

*Coco-Cola and Brotherhood*

# Pickers

No one picks their nose
quite like a man at a red light.
Red for the sake of safety.
Recently free
from the inanity
of surviving home. Driving
just to drive away.
It hardly matters where,
when or how. The sky is crumbling,
the road is littered with
like-minded pedestrians—
all pickers of their own causes,
their own weighted cases,
making the best of time.
And who wouldn't
want to clean house
at a crossroads?
Now that he is alone
or pretending to be.
And happy. And already
missing those he's promised
to miss. Rolling down the window,
the scattered dark telling him
to raise his voice.
And turn around. Now,
before the rain begins in earnest.
And the gathering clouds
explode with crows.

# Confronting Plagiarism

*Frostburg University*

You expect tears, groveling,
but not the impossible truth spoken
with convincing pathos by one
Mindy Gillian, genius of English 101.
That it is they who stole from *her*—
How Goethe—lost soul that he is—crept
into her dorm, onto her computer,
how Darwin discovered her essay
on the internet, wrote *Origin of Species*
without once citing her. Never mind
the needed time travel, we'd figure that out later.
What we wanted now was action.
We were both angry and near crying.
And because I knew the cost
of consequence, the inevitable disaster
if we let this thing get out of hand,
I advised her to sue hard and fast.
I'd prepare the paperwork myself.
With the help of the University's Judicial Committee
we'd get Confucius on that witness stand,
mere bones now, to shed his tears of desperate dust
for sweet Mindy Gillian's vast intellect.
Only a matter of time before we'd break
Virgil together. Squeeze Sophocles dry.
Stop Plato's ridiculous rape of Gillian's third paper,
the argumentative essay. It's embarrassing—
to unearth Shakespeare, once legend,
only to expel him, if we have any scruples at all,
from the entire Maryland School System, forever.

# Inner City English

*North Philadelphia, Mastbaum High School*

Students skip through Whitman's Brooklyn,
Bradstreet's fire—that Anglo-Saxon vision
of violence—and teacher teaches and Puritans
pray for an answer from an angry God
and below the screaming of early American literature,
the sound of pens pirouetting the paper stage.
Now I remember why I took this job.
Everyone is on task, even Idrees, who I know I'll fail.
And though he has forgotten his pen and paper, his head is up
which, believe me, is a step forward.
Rhianna, who forgets her journal every day,
has borrowed the needed supplies, answers today's
essential question. Yesterday's speech has worked: Respect
and quiet and raising your hand and love
for your peers and blossoming community and I am walking
around the room in awe when almost predictably,
Diamond drops her book, turns to Lavelle,
who cannot quell his laughter and intones:
"Get your motherfucking hands off
my fucking body. I. Will. Fuck. You. Up."
Rhianna and the rest, in choreographed time,
look from Diamond, who knows she's right, to me,
their reluctant leader. No one's head is down.
Everyone listens. They wait. They want to know who I really am.

## Simile

The High School curriculum allows 4 weeks
on Epic Convention, 2 weeks grammar instruction,

and 8 weeks on figurative language, though
it is clear to me, when walking through those

harried halls, that these teenagers are already masters.
While the metaphor is a question, apostrophe a struggle,

imagery dead on arrival, they have clearly mastered
the simile, a device by now so familiar, they hardly recognize

their own astute perfection of comparison.
Outside, it is cold as shit. Inside, hot as shit.

You may be smart as shit or dumb as shit.
Some are mad as shit, bad as shit, tough as shit

and scared as shit. There is no end, apparently,
to what shit is or is not, can or cannot do.

According to some of my brightest, shit
is both heavy and light, loud, soft, far and fat.

Though, for reasons too obvious to clarify,
you will never hear disgusting as shit, brown as shit,

or smelly as shit. Why weigh shit down
with what is already evident?

Give it the freedom of expression without which
it is lost as shit. Running behind schedule? Late as shit.

Missed lunch? Hungry as shit. Don't think shit
is capable of jealousy? Horniness? Sloth?

This is not your grandmother's shit.
Look it up: Pg. 37. Strunk and White. Class dismissed.

# Renaldo

On a day when the snow
blankets the emergency of
North East Philadelphia
like Nina Simone
blankets depression,
I tell a student, barely 16,
*Good Luck,* when he tells me,
with a smile in his voice,
he wants to become
a doctor. He thinks this
is what I want to hear.
And I haven't yet
gotten his joke: I am white.
And privileged. Grew up
with both parents
talking to me,
never worried about shoes,
flew to Greece and Germany,
paid for prom.
I've given him 50 points
for completing the essay:
"My Five Year Plan."
The bell rings but he remains
in his seat for what seems
a long time, looking at me.
I look at him too,
though soon I move
to my desk. The door is open.
Another class begins
to enter. But Renaldo remains:
This boy who I can't
get to class on time, now,
will not leave. He stands
and says, "Mister, I live in the ghetto,"
and closes the door, gently,
the way one would
when a sleeping baby
is in the room, so slowly.
No chance of waking it.

## To the Jules E. Mastbaum High School Student Who Positioned Me 8th on His Hit List.

My parents divorced too, Nathan.
I learned to unlove those who needed
my love most. And if you think I don't ask
everyday what songs I'd sing if they'd stayed
together, you'd be right. But only because
I have different worries now. My wife and I
plan to buy a house. On our income,
and what with sky-rocketing New Jersey property taxes,
we can't afford a quiet street. But to cut our own grass,
to feed a child everything we know to be real!
Look, I've wished for someone to hold me too.
For a father who is proud to call me son, a mother
who wants me despite what I became without her.
How many relationships have I murdered
through my own ignorance and loneliness
and fear of being called coward? Death
by death, the same angel devours us both.
But let's reevaluate this thing here.
Surely I've earned the top five. Yesterday's
comment alone about your imprisoned skank
of a mother should have put me into the top two. C'mon.
I'm top two material. I suppose this is my ego talking,
but I thought we were tighter than that.
Give me another chance, Nathan. Let me tell you what I really think.

# When You're Late

It always means death
for the mind is never reasonable.
Some side-burned psychopath
has raped you repeatedly in
a brush patch off the bypass. You
walking to your car, he splitting
your lower lip, taking your keys
and phone. Or else you lie
on a highway embankment with
a broken leg, a concussion pending,
believing your name is Alice,
unable to tell the emergency crew
where you live because you're squawking
Hebrew, begging for soup. At 4 minutes late,
it is I who must tell your parents, my parents,
our daughter, your second cousin in Minneapolis,
the people you've meant to call for weeks, what happened.
6 minutes late and I am making funeral arrangements,
determining how much and who will speak, will it be an open casket
or closed, figuring out how to raise Mayzie alone, until one day,
(7 minutes late) the possibility of remarriage, if there is remarriage,
which there won't be, no one else will have me, I will have no one else,
not when you're 8 minutes late and I know that Mayzie and I will spend
our lives in matching knit sweaters embroidered with a picture
of you skipping rope. At 12 minutes late I'm rearranging
my work schedule so I can take her to school in the morning,
if school is appropriate, which, maybe it's not, they'll understand,
and how will I pick her up from school, by learning to drive the bus,
that's how, becoming reluctant PTSA President, chaperoning
every field trip to the Baltimore aquarium and at 13 minutes late
I am on the phone with your parents asking them to consider
the east coast, to raise Mayzie as a Jew and who are you to tell me
you'd be home at 7:30 when it's already 7:32, 33, 34, 35.

## After Reading Grace Paley, I'm Inspired to Write a Short Poem

Why some die and others stay,
I don't know.
Only the taste of declamation
the living pass between them:
*We should see each other soon*
*before this happens again.*

Four years pass.

Your mother describes your father
as stubborn, consuming, irreplaceable.
Your hold back your tears like a professional.

# Walking In

Have you too been victimized
by a tall, plainspoken, overdressed
stranger, a zealous pre-teen,
an overweight middle-aged graybeard
opening the bathroom door
you thought you locked, as you sit
on the can, pants tight to ankles,
underwear couched in pants,
pushing, pushing? I'm talking
about the delicacy of doors,
an unreliable inch of brittle bolt,
the distraction of those with whom
we share the earth. I'm talking about
the fragility of our social contract:
a Thanksgiving day grocery store, for instance,
a Black Friday Target. Or else at home,
with your back turned: perhaps you are the type
to close your eyes, bury your flushed face
in a reader's digest. Whatever your posture,
debilitating, awkward, slack jawed shock
turned stutter awaits when footsteps
approach, one, then another
and the slow turn of the knob
catches you without. Even with the territorial
cough, the warning flush, the stamping of feet,
we are the lost, sudden emptying of trees,
the student called upon to answer
without an answer. And then again, maybe you
have been the one on the other side, who,
for post-lunch purposes, time constraints,
a general lack of spacial acuity
have refused to recognize what is in front of you.
What use a knob, you reason, if not meant
to turn? And our failed rules of governance,
our negation of civil construct
plunges us once more into savagery,
the stooping of backs, the returning to caves.

## Peeing After the Movie

Even if the film was everything
you wanted—the slow, awkward,
man-child admitting to love,
the three sisters realizing
what they must accomplish
before midnight—this is still
the most satisfying scene, half-running
to the john through the awakening dark,
trying to hold yourself in, trying
hard to be dignified, then, once
the line in front of you has passed,
dropping your pants, feeling
the world wrap its forgiveness,
once again, around you.
What an ending—something only Hollywood
could produce: surrounded
by your fellow hedonists—
a community of the happiest strangers
you've ever had the privilege
to relieve yourself next to. See the white tile
shining, hear the echoing sounds
of satisfaction, the knowledge that
god is still possible, looking us in the eye,
reminding us what a little Coca-Cola
and brotherhood, once combined, can yield.

The New York Quarterly Foundation, Inc.

New York, New York

## Poetry Magazine

**Since 1969**

Edgy, fresh, groundbreaking, eclectic—voices from all walks of life.

Definitely NOT your mama's poetry magazine!

The *New York Quarterly* has been defining the term contemporary American poetry since its first craft interview with W. H. Auden.

Interviews • Essays • and of course, lots of poems.

**www.nyq.org**

No contest! That's correct, NYQ Books are NO CONTEST to other small presses because we do not support ourselves through contests. Our books are carefully selected by invitation only, so you know that NYQ Books are produced with the same editorial integrity as the magazine that has brought you the most eclectic contemporary American poetry since 1969.

## Books

**www.nyq.org**

poetry at the edge™

www.ingramcontent.com/pod-product-compliance
Lightning Source LLC
LaVergne TN
LVHW041344080426
835512LV00006B/605